A·GUIDED EXPERIENCE

SHADOW WORK

JOURNAL

Shadow Work Journal: Alchemy of the Hidden Self

2025 fEMPOWER Press Trade Paperback Edition
Copyright © 2025 JESSICA CALLERY

Published in Canada, for Global Distribution by fEMPOWER Publications
www.fempower.pub | For more information email: media@fempower.pub

ISBN trade paperback: 978-1-998721-20-7

To order additional copies of this book: media@fempower.pub

A GUIDED EXPERIENCE

SHADOW WORK

JOURNAL

ALCHEMY OF THE HIDDEN SELF

JESSICA CALLERY

UNDERNEATH the surface of our being, our bones, our skin, lies a portal untouched by light. The shadow is where lost wounds, silenced desires, and untamed truths quietly reside. Shadow work is the spiritual art of turning inward, of sinking into this inner twilight not to defeat, but to listen. Here in the shadow, in muffled honesty, we meet the parts of ourselves we have banished. Yet it is here we have the power to find the keys to our totality. Through this valiant alchemy, pain softens, shame transforms into wisdom, and what once felt broken begins to return home. In submerging into the darkness, we do not become lost but found. The shadow does not dim the light; rather, it clarifies it. When we can be so bold to face it, we then rise, full and true.

INTRODUCTION:
THE POWER OF THE SHADOW

Within each of us lives a shadow, the unconscious part of our psyche where we store repressed emotions, forgotten memories, and parts of ourselves we've deemed unworthy, unlovable, or dangerous.

Shadow work is the courageous act of turning inward to explore these buried parts, not to judge or fix them, but to understand and reclaim them. Through this sacred process, we transform pain into wisdom, fear into freedom, and shame into authenticity. Shadow work is not self-improvement—it's self-reclamation.

HOW TO
USE THIS JOURNAL

This journal is a space for deep truth-telling. There is no right or wrong way to move through it—one only needs honesty, presence, and a willingness to feel. To get the most from this journal:

Δ Create a safe, quiet space where you won't be interrupted.

Δ Move slowly. Power is in the stillness.

Δ Be honest. You're not here to be perfect; you're here to be real.

Δ Use your body as a guide. Pay attention to where emotions live—breathe into those spaces.

Δ Return to your entries. Rereading them over time may reveal deeper truths.

MEANING
OF THE LOTUS

SECTION 1:

THE LOTUS FLOWER

To carry the inner child, the grief, the flame,
To now love when at one time you learned to shame.

The lotus ascends not despite
But throughout the dark, it seeks the light
A paradox in every part
The mud and dirt below the open heart.

So unearth, descend, don't turn away,
Your truth is born in hues of gray
And when you bloom, you'll understand
Your roots still hold you

The mud is not the culmination but the start
The shadow's gift is an overflowing heart.

The lotus flower is a powerful and ancient symbol found in many cultures, particularly in Eastern philosophies and spiritual traditions. It often represents purity, rebirth, spiritual awakening, and enlightenment, especially because it grows in muddy, murky water yet blooms into something beautiful and clean above the surface.

MEANING
OF THE LOTUS:

△ Resilience and Growth: The lotus roots itself in mud
(difficulty, darkness) but rises toward the light.

△ Purity and Detachment: Despite growing in filth, it remains
unstained, symbolizing purity and the ability to rise above
worldly suffering.

△ Spiritual Emergence: In many cultures and religions, it's
a metaphor for the soul's journey—through suffering and
ignorance (mud) into awareness and liberation (bloom).

△ Cycles and Transformation: The opening and closing of
the flower reflect cycles of life, death, and rebirth.

CORRELATION TO SHADOW WORK:

Shadow work is the process of exploring the hidden or unconscious parts of ourselves—our "shadow." This includes repressed emotions, fears, trauma, and behaviors we deem unacceptable.

Here's how the lotus connects to shadow work:

LOTUS SYMBOLISM	SHADOW WORK
Grows in mud	You face your inner darkness or wounds
Rises through water	You process and feel the depth of those emotions
Blooms in light	You emerge with awareness, healing, and self-acceptance
Untouched by filth	You learn that darkness doesn't define your worth but is rather a part of the path to wholeness

In essence, just as the lotus needs mud to bloom, we often need to confront and embrace our shadow in order to truly grow, heal, and evolve.

SHADOW WORK JOURNAL PROMPTS: FROM MUD TO BLOOM

WHAT ARE THE "MUDDY WATERS" IN MY LIFE RIGHT NOW?

Reflect on the painful, messy, or suppressed emotions, memories, or patterns you often avoid.

HOW HAVE THESE SHADOWS SHAPED ME—POSITIVELY OR NEGATIVELY?

Consider how these difficult parts of you may have also built resilience, insight, or compassion.

WHAT WOULD IT LOOK LIKE TO "GROW THROUGH" THIS INSTEAD OF AVOIDING IT?

Imagine a version of yourself that uses this pain

as a catalyst for growth or healing.

WHAT DOES MY "BLOOM" LOOK LIKE?

Visualize the qualities, mindset, or life you are working toward by embracing your shadow.

HOW CAN I HOLD SPACE
FOR BOTH THE MUD AND THE
FLOWER WITHIN ME?

Write a short affirmation or intention that honors your wholeness. Don't overthink it, just allow the words to flow.

"I am the lotus born of the dirt, formed by shadows,
yet ascending always toward the light. I do not dread the darkness,
for it is the soil of my becoming."

–Jessica Callery

MEANING
OF THE EVIL EYE

SECTION 2: EVIL EYE

THE GAZE
AND THE GLASS

In stillness, the shadow stirs, veiled in contempt

A gaze that creeps, covet reborn.

Not just an oath from those who loathe

But a mirror held under your own mask.

Evil eye is not just that of theirs

It's the gaze we ignite from unhealed layers.

Shadow-born thoughts, unfulfilled desires,

Powering concealed, inner fires.

That gaze, afraid, from others we hide

Yet neglect the poison we hold inside

Every wound we ignore and won't explore

Unlocks within us a darker door

Shadow work is an art of sight

Toward claiming our own darkness in honest light.

To encounter the eye not as enemy

But as the part of us that brings harmony.

So, let the eye not taint but teach

That healing lies in digging deep.

For when we recognize what lies beneath

We shatter the spell, we learn to breathe.

The evil eye represents both a symbol of harm caused by negative energy—often envy, jealousy, or malice—and a deeper metaphor for the power of unseen energy between people.

THE EVIL EYE & SHADOW WORK: A SPIRITUAL MIRROR

ASPECT	SPIRITUAL MEANING	CONNECTION TO SHADOW WORK
Evil Eye as a Curse or Projection	Δ Jealousy/envy projected onto others Δ Can cause energetic harm (intentionally or unintentionally)	Δ Reflects our own unhealed envy or resentment Δ Invites us to notice when we feel threatened by others' success
Evil Eye as Protection	Δ Used in jewelry, amulets deflect negative energy Δ A symbol of energetic boundaries	Δ Represents the need to create healthy boundaries Δ A reminder to honor our energetic space without closing off emotionally
Power of Intention & Energy	Δ Emotions and thoughts carry vibrational energy Δ What we project affects others and ourselves	Δ Highlights the importance of self-awareness Δ Encourages examining how unconscious feelings may ripple outward
Fear of Being Seen	Δ Fear of attracting envy Δ Fear of judgment or "evil eye" from others	Δ Points to insecurities or wounds we haven't healed Δ Reveals fear of being "too much" or "not enough"
Spiritual Invitation	Δ Balance between protection and openness Δ Use the symbol to heal not just guard	

SHADOW WORK JOURNAL PROMPTS: THE EYE AND THE MIRROR

WHERE IN MY LIFE DO I
FEEL JUDGED? HOW DOES THIS
AFFECT MY SENSE OF SELF?

Explore where you feel exposed,
criticized, or compared—and how that impacts
your behavior or confidence.

WHEN HAVE I CAST THE "EVIL EYE"—
FELT JEALOUSY, RESENTMENT,
OR SILENT BITTERNESS TOWARD
SOMEONE ELSE? WHAT WAS I TRULY
YEARNING FOR IN THOSE MOMENTS?

Reflect on moments of envy or quiet resentment.

WHAT PARTS OF ME DO I HIDE BECAUSE
I'M AFRAID THEY WILL BE JUDGED
OR MISUNDERSTOOD? WHO TAUGHT ME
TO FEAR BEING FULLY SEEN?

Identify the parts of yourself you suppress out of fear.

Consider who made you feel unsafe being your full self.

DO I FEAR SUCCESS, BEAUTY,
OR ABUNDANCE BECAUSE I WORRY IT
WILL ATTRACT ENVY OR NEGATIVITY?
WHAT SHADOW BELIEF LIVES
UNDER THAT FEAR?

Examine any fear of "shining too brightly."

What belief about success, attention,

or safety lives beneath it?

IF THE EVIL EYE IS A MIRROR,
WHAT IS IT TRYING TO SHOW ME
ABOUT UNHEALED PARTS OF MYSELF?
WHAT EMOTION OR MEMORY
WANTS TO BE WITNESSED?

Use the symbol of the evil eye as a reflection of your inner world. What wounds or emotions are being triggered when you feel judged or seen?

WHERE AM I STILL PERFORMING FOR
PROTECTION—WEARING A VERSION OF
MYSELF TO DEFLECT OTHERS' GAZE
OR OPINIONS? WHO WOULD
I BE WITHOUT THAT MASK?

Reflect on the personas you adopt
to stay safe or accepted.

WHAT WOULD IT LOOK LIKE TO
TRANSFORM ENVY—MINE OR ANOTH-
ER'S—INTO A PORTAL FOR DEEPER
UNDERSTANDING AND CONNECTION?

Instead of rejecting envy, use it as insight. What can it
teach you about your desires or unmet needs?

HOW CAN I PROTECT MY ENERGY
WHILE ALSO REMAINING OPEN
AND AUTHENTIC? WHAT BOUNDARIES
OR RITUALS WOULD SUPPORT
THAT BALANCE?

Balance protection and vulnerability with practices
that help you stay grounded and open-hearted
without absorbing others' projections.

MEANING OF THE
THE MOON

SECTION 3: THE MOON

M O O N S K I N

The Moon acquaints with

What the Sun cannot graze
The sting beneath your smile

The tale you silence
When the world views
She rises

Not to unsee

But to reveal

the glimmers of truth

in the concealed corner of your soul

she teaches with no words

that you do not need to be intact

to be admirable

only honest.

In her glow,

your shadows are not demons

just memories

waiting to be understood,

afflictions craving light gentle enough

to stay.

She does not hurry.

She mirrors.

She echoes.

She listens

And in her flow,

you are reminded:

recovery is not linear.

It's lunar.

The Moon holds rich symbolic meaning across spiritual traditions, often representing the inner world, the feminine, and the cyclical nature of life.

THE MOON: A SPIRITUAL MIRROR OF THE INNER SELF

THEME	SPIRITUAL MEANING	REFLECTION OR INSIGHT
The Inner Self & Emotions	Governs the unconscious mind, intuition, and emotions	Reveals the ebb and flow of feelings, hidden patterns, and deep desires
Divine Feminine Energy	Embodies receptivity, nurturing, creativity, and mystery	Honors rest, reflection, and inner knowing—balances the Sun's active masculine energy
Cycles & Change	The Moon's phases reflect the nonlinear nature of life	Symbolizes transformation, letting go, and permission to move through phases
Illumination of the Shadow	Reflects light rather than producing it—symbolizing self-reflection	Helps gently reveal our shadow traits, hidden truths, and unconscious behaviors
Connection to the Subconscious & Sacred	Linked to rituals, magic, and the unseen realms	A gateway to spiritual insight; often used during phases for cleansing and intention
The Moon as a Mirror	Reflects the soul's inner landscape and natural rhythm	A teacher of quiet wisdom, emotional truth, and the beauty of darkness

SHADOW WORK
JOURNAL PROMPTS:
NEW MOON-
THE VOID/NEW
BEGINNINGS

WHAT PART OF ME FEELS HIDDEN
OR LOST? WHAT WANTS TO BE
BORN FROM THAT VOID?

Explore the parts of you that feel uncertain,
numb, or "missing." Often, emptiness is fertile
ground for transformation.

WHAT HAVE I BEEN AFRAID
TO START BECAUSE I DON'T YET
FEEL "WHOLE ENOUGH"?

Notice where perfectionism or self-doubt
delays your growth. What dream is waiting for
your permission, not your perfection?

WHAT EMOTIONS OR TRUTHS ARE
BEGINNING TO SURFACE, EVEN IN
SMALL WAYS? HOW CAN I MAKE
SPACE FOR THEM TO GROW?

This is the space of sacred noticing—where the soul speaks
softly, and you learn to listen. Honor what arises, even in
fragments, and let it bloom in its own time.

WHEN HAVE I FELT LIKE I HAD TO
CHANGE PARTS OF MYSELF TO GAIN
APPROVAL OR STAY SAFE? WHAT WOULD
RECLAIMING THEM LOOK LIKE?

Invite your hidden selves back into the light,
not in shame, but in sacred reclamation. You no longer
shrink to fit in—you expand to become whole.

WHAT IS THE TRUTH I'M AVOIDING BECAUSE IT MIGHT CHANGE EVERYTHING?

To meet this truth is to welcome transformation.

It may unravel what you know—but in its wake,

it offers liberation.

WHAT PATTERNS KEEP REPEATING IN MY LIFE—AND WHAT SHADOW BELIEF MIGHT BE FUELING THEM?

With loving awareness, trace the thread of repetition back to its root. Don't shame the pattern, learn from it. Then, choose again.

WHAT PART OF MY IDENTITY FEELS HEAVY OR FALSE—READY TO BE RELEASED?

Like old skin, it once protected you. But now, it constricts.
Bless it, release it, and return to your authentic essence.

WHAT EMOTIONAL WEIGHT HAVE I
CARRIED THAT NO LONGER
BELONGS TO ME? WHAT WOULD
IT FEEL LIKE TO LAY IT DOWN?

This is the sacred act of surrender—laying down
the weight at the altar of truth.

WHAT DOES SILENCE TEACH ME ABOUT
MYSELF? WHAT TRUTHS COME UP
WHEN I STOP PERFORMING, STRIVING,
OR EXPLAINING?

When you stop performing, striving,

or explaining, the soul speaks clearly.

Silence is not empty, it is full of knowing.

WHAT AM I INTEGRATING RIGHT NOW— WHAT WISDOM HAVE MY SHADOWS OFFERED ME?

Think of the moments when you struggled, stumbled, or felt lost. What did you learn about yourself? Shadows are soil for transformation. Think about the lessons your pain has taught you, the strength born from your struggles, how your past coping has shaped your current truth, and how embracing these lessons is reshaping who you are becoming.

SAY OUT LOUD
IN THE MIRROR:

As I close these pages, I honor the journey I've taken through the shadows of my own soul.

This journal was not a search for perfection but a brave return to wholeness. I've faced the parts of me that were once hidden, denied, or feared—and in doing so, I have begun to reclaim them with compassion.

Shadow work isn't about becoming someone new. It's about remembering who I've always been beneath the layers: honest, complex, worthy, and real.

Some truths were hard to hold. Some wounds asked for gentleness, not judgment. But I showed up—for all of it. And that is enough.

As I move forward, I carry this truth:
My shadows are not my weakness—they are my teachers.
And light doesn't make me whole.
The courage to see myself fully does.

This is not an ending.
It's an integration.
A soft, sacred beginning.

THE LIGHT I FOUND IN THE DARK

I recorded this journal
not to correct myself
but to meet the parts
I drowned with a hush.

Here, I sat with my shadows
not as foes
but as angels

Each hurt became a whisper,
each fear a cord
leading back to honesty and truth.

And though the light was dim

At times flickering
it was mine

born from the dark I dared to meet.

Now, I carry this light

I carry this light in my being
Not over me
but within me.

Not to shine over the rest
but to evoke to myself
I am full
even in pieces.

And healing
was never about becoming someone new
it was always

Always, always
about remembering
who I was from the start.

Jessica Callery is a best-selling author, spiritual mentor, and devoted mom of two. A sobriety advocate with lived experience in addiction and recovery, she guides others through healing  and transformation by blending spirituality, intuition, and shadow work. Her work centers on manifestation, alignment, emotional resilience, and awakening to inner guidance. With a mission to help people return to their true essence, Jessica empowers her clients to experience profound shifts and create lives of clarity, connection, and purpose.

@iamjesscallery
@jessicacallerycoaching
www.jessicacallery.ca

fEMPOWER
PUBLICATIONS

At fEMPOWER Publications,
we don't just publish books—we amplify movements.

We support thought leaders, visionary storytellers, and creative entrepreneurs
in transforming their ideas into powerful nonfiction books, journals, workbooks,
affirmation decks, and personal growth tools that leave lasting impact.

Our mission is to help our authors protect their soul's work, expand HER platform
beyond the page, and turn HER message into a timeless legacy.

www.fempower.pub | @fempower.pub ⊙

www.ingramcontent.com/pod-product-compliance
Lightning Source LLC
Chambersburg PA
CBHW051303120626
46547CB00015B/2065